TERRORIST ATTACKS

THE ATTACK AGAINST THE U.S. EMBASSIES IN KENYA AND TANZANIA

Amanda Ferguson

The Rosen Publishing Group, Inc.
New York

Published in 2003 by The Rosen Publishing Group, Inc.
29 East 21st Street, New York, NY 10010

First Edition

Library of Congress Cataloging-in-Publication Data

Ferguson, Amanda.
The attack against the U.S. embassies in Kenya and Tanzania / By Amanda Ferguson. — 1st ed.
  p. cm. — (Terrorist attacks)
Includes bibliographical references and index.
Summary: An account of the bombings of the U.S. Embassies in Kenya and Tanzania, discussing the motives behind the bombings, events surrounding these acts of terror, and the trial of the men involved.
ISBN 0-8239-3652-X (lib. bdg.)
1. United States Embassy Bombing, Nairobi, Kenya, 1998—Juvenile literature.
2. United States Embassy Bombing, Dar es Salaam, Tanzania, 1998—Juvenile literature. 3. Bombings—Kenya—Nairobi—Juvenile literature. 4. Bombings--Tanzania—Dar es Salaam—Juvenile literature. 5. Terrorism—United States—Juvenile literature. 6. Trials (Terrorism)—United States—Juvenile literature.
[1. United States Embassy Bombing, Nairobi, Kenya, 1998. 2. United States Embassy Bombing, Dar es Salaam, Tanzania, 1998. 3. Terrorism.]
I. Title: Attack against the United States embassies in Kenya and Tanzania.
II. Title. III. Series.
HV6433.K4 F47 2002
967.62'5042--dc21
                                                    2001007608

CONTENTS

INTRODUCTION

On August 7, 1998, a man walking near the United States Embassy in Nairobi, Kenya, heard a thump. He didn't know what the noise was or where it was coming from. Then he heard a blast. Glass windows blew in and flames roared out of the stately embassy building. A block away, a businessman heard the explosion. He ran out into the street and looked up at the sky. "All you could see were thousands of files flying though the air," he told *U.S. News and World Report.* "It was nothing but paper, dust and darkness." At virtually the same moment, 450 miles away in Dar es Salaam, Tanzania, a car bomb exploded outside the U.S. Embassy.

Scorched buildings; burning cars; charred, twisted metal; bloody bodies—the bombings were brutal. Hundreds of people were killed, including twelve U.S. citizens. Thousands were seriously wounded. Many died later from their injuries. Before the week was over, newspapers around the world were calling the twin bombings a terrorist attack.

Terrorism

Terrorism is a type of political violence intended to frighten a particular group of people. The word comes from the Latin word *terrere*, meaning "to cause to tremble." It first came into use as a political term during the French Revolution at the end of the eighteenth century. Today, terrorist acts refer mainly to public acts of destruction. Often committed anonymously, without any clear military objective, the seemingly random acts lead to fear and panic. Terrorists want people to wonder who would do such things, and why. They want people to fear that they might be the next targets.

For almost fifty years, until the end of the Cold War (1945–1991), the United States government focused its military power against the Soviet Union and Communism. Now that the Cold War is over and the Soviet Union is no longer an enemy, the United States faces a new threat: terrorism.

Terrorism has a long tradition in world history. From ancient times to the present, revolutionaries have used terrorist tactics to overthrow governments. Religious crusaders have used violence to force others to abandon their religious beliefs and practices. Today's terrorists have a variety of religious and political agendas. Some terrorists are willing to sacrifice their lives in order to make their point.

Terrorists do not view their actions the same way their opponents do. They see their actions as heroic and virtuous. Some Muslim extremists regard suicide bombing as a noble act for which they will be rewarded in the afterlife. This kind of violence is especially difficult to combat: Is it possible to compromise with those who believe so strongly in their cause that they are willing to kill and die for it?

A Kenyan soldier prepares to raise the American flag outside the U.S. Embassy in Nairobi.

Today the Federal Bureau of Investigation (FBI) recognizes two types of terrorism in the United States: domestic and international. Both types have threatened the United States. Early in the twentieth century, some labor leaders used violence to show their commitment to revolutionary philosophies. They wanted to get rid of a government they felt was corrupt. In the 1960s and early 1970s, groups such as the Weather Underground Organization bombed buildings to protest U.S. involvement in the Vietnam War. Between 1978 and 1995, an anarchist known as the Unabomber mailed bombs that killed and wounded several people throughout the United States. In April 1995 a truck bomb exploded in front of the Alfred P. Murrah Federal Building in Oklahoma City, Oklahoma, killing 168 people and injuring more than 500. At the time, it was the deadliest terrorist attack in United States history. Timothy McVeigh and Terry Nichols, two extremists, were charged and sentenced for the crime. They attacked because they believed the U.S. government had too much control over individuals.

Terrorism is widespread partly because it is practical. Terrorists don't need large armies to attack their enemies. They don't need much money or sophisticated weapons to blow up a building or plane, or to take people hostage. They can act alone, without the help or cooperation of other nations. If a terrorist operation is successful, political gain can be high. Regimes can weaken or fall. If a terrorist operation fails, the terrorists' loss is relatively minor. Because terrorist groups operate in secret, it is difficult for nations to defend themselves or retaliate.

In 1996, President Bill Clinton signed antiterrorism legislation to strengthen the power of the federal government to deal with terrorism. The law made it illegal for groups to raise funds for terrorism. It called for the death penalty in cases of international terrorism. The law allows U.S. officials to deport foreign terrorists without having to disclose evidence against them. It authorized up to $1 billion for state and local antiterrorism efforts. Both the American Civil Liberties Union (ACLU) and the National Rifle Association (NRA) opposed parts of the legislation. They claimed it gave the federal government too much power, and that it could violate citizens' rights.

The day after the attacks on the African embassies, a group calling itself the Islamic Army for the Liberation of Holy Places claimed responsibility. They pledged new attacks on U.S. targets. The name of the group was new to U.S. officials, but terrorism in the name of Islam wasn't.

A marine guards the U.S. Embassy in Nairobi, which was blown apart by Islamic terrorists.

ISLAM'S HOLY WAR

CHAPTER 1

A plane is hijacked in Paris. A bomb explodes in a Jerusalem shopping mall. A group of tourists is gunned down in front of an Egyptian temple. A plane full of holiday travelers is blown up over Scotland. Over the past three decades, many such incidents have been linked with Islamic terrorists.

Islam is a major world religion that was founded in Arabia. Those who follow Islam are called Muslims. There are over one billion Muslims in the world today. Islam has flourished in a variety of regions. The major groups that make up the Islamic community include Arabs in

Devout Muslims must face Mecca and pray five times a day. There are about 1.3 billion Muslims in the world, compared with 2 billion Christians and about 14 million Jews.

North Africa and the Middle East; sub-Saharan Africans; Turks in Turkey and Central Asia; Iranians; Afghans; South Asians in Pakistan, India, and Bangladesh; Southeast Asians in Malaysia, Indonesia, and the Philippines; and a small percentage of Chinese. In Europe, Islam is the second largest religion after Christianity. Currently, Islam is growing in popularity in the United States.

Muslims believe in one god, Allah. According to Islam, the ultimate purpose of humanity is to worship Allah and build a society free of corruption. Muslims believe that peace can be achieved by obeying the teachings of the Arab prophet Mohammed. Mohammed lived from AD 570–632. When

Mohammed was forty years old, he began to preach Islam as the true religion. Islam considers Mohammed to be God's last prophet. Muslims believe Mohammed received divine revelations and these are collected in a sacred text called the Koran.

Islamic fundamentalists rigidly obey the teachings of the Koran. They are generally opposed to Western society. Many believe that giving social and political freedom to women leads to moral decay and social ruin. Some fundamentalists are suspicious of democracy because they do not trust the morals of the masses. They feel that leaders in some Muslim countries have not done enough to help their poor and rapidly growing populations. Perhaps most important, many fundamentalists bitterly resent Western colonialism. It has made them regard everything Western as evil.

Jihad is usually translated as "holy war." It refers to the Islamic goal of "reforming one's base nature" and also society. Jihad may include the use of armed force, if necessary. In the last century, the concept of Jihad has inspired many Muslims in their struggle against Western colonialism.

The word "Islam" comes from the Arabic word *salama*, which means "peace." The Muslim way of life is mostly peaceful. Mohammad's central teachings focus on the unity of God and the need for generosity and justice in human relations. Most Muslims say that the extremists who carry out violent acts in the name of Allah are not Islamic and should not be thought of as Islamic. They stress that these groups of terrorists do not speak for the majority of Muslims.

Osama bin Laden

It is believed that Osama bin Laden was behind the attacks on the U.S. Embassies in Kenya and Tanzania. His network of terrorists was also responsible for the September 11, 2001, terror attacks on the World Trade Center in New York City and the Pentagon in Washington, D.C.

Saudi Arabian multimillionaire Osama bin Laden is thought to be the mastermind behind many terrorist acts. He is not the only instigator of terrorist attacks on behalf of Islam, but he is the most infamous. Bin Laden's money and followers have been linked to attacks as far-flung as Tajikistan in Central Asia, Bosnia and Chechnya in Europe, Sudan in Africa, and New York City. His devotion to Islam and his role in organizing thousands of Arab volunteers to battle the Soviets in Afghanistan in the 1980s have made him a popular figure in the Islamic world.

Born in 1957, Osama bin Laden is the youngest surviving son of one of Saudi Arabia's wealthiest families. When he was a young man, he was a free spirit and did many things that go against the teachings of Islam. In 1979, three events made bin Laden want to become active in politics: Egypt signed a peace treaty with Israel; the Soviet

Union invaded the Muslim nation of Afghanistan; and revolutionaries overthrew the Shah of Iran. Bin Laden believed these events threatened Islam. He joined other Arabs to fight the powerful Soviets. Because the men were fighting Communist takeover, the U.S. government considered them "freedom fighters." The United States secretly gave the men money, weapons, and training as an investment against the spread of Communism.

When Soviet troops left Afghanistan, bin Laden returned to Saudi Arabia. He criticized Saudi Arabia's regime and was exiled. His family renounced him. He was thrown out of Saudi Arabia just as U.S. troops were arriving for the Persian Gulf War in 1991. The presence of the U.S. government infuriated bin Laden. He saw U.S. troops in Saudi Arabia as militant invaders trying to replace Islamic governments with corrupt, nonreligious governments.

BIN LADEN NETWORK

Osama bin Laden is rumored to have a network of several thousand allies. Many are Arabs who fought the Soviet invasion of Afghanistan from 1979 to 1989. After the Soviets left Afghanistan, many of bin Laden's followers returned to their home countries. They created an alliance of "holy warriors" in North Africa, the Middle East, and Central Asia. Groups who signed bin Laden's *fatwa*, or holy ruling, calling for the killing of Americans include the Islamic Jihad (Egypt), Gamaa Islamiya (Egypt), and Harkat ul-Ansar (Pakistan).

"JIHAD AGAINST JEWS AND CRUSADERS"

World Islamic Front Statement, February 23, 1998

The Arabian Peninsula has never—since God made it flat, created its desert, and encircled it with seas—been stormed by any forces like the crusader armies spreading in it like locusts, eating its riches and wiping out its plantations. All this is happening at a time in which nations are attacking Muslims like people fighting over a plate of food. In the light of the grave situation and the lack of support . . . we should all agree on how to settle the matter.

The ruling to kill the Americans and their allies—civilians and military—is an individual duty for every Muslim who can do it, in order to liberate the al-Aqsa Mosque and the holy mosque [Mecca] from their grip, and in order for their armies to move out of all the lands of Islam, defeated and unable to threaten any Muslim. This is in accordance with the words of Almighty God, "and fight them until there is no tumult or oppression, and there prevail justice and faith in God."

Bin Laden moved to Sudan, where he is said to have run numerous terrorist training camps. In 1996, under pressure from the United States and Saudi Arabia, the Sudanese government asked bin Laden to leave.

Bin Laden returned to Afghanistan. The country's new, Islamic fundamentalist government, the Taliban, welcomed him. In exchange for their support, bin Laden gave the fledgling government money. Thanks to his riches, he was free to continue to plan his terrorist campaigns from Afghanistan.

Islamic guerrilla fighters crouch on a hill in Afghanistan.

Extremists such as bin Laden believe that terrorist acts are justified because U.S. foreign policy has led to the deaths of Arabs. They want to rid the Middle East of Western influence. They believe that Muslims are under American attack. They resent U.S. military and political presence in the Middle East and feel that American culture is corrupting the world.

In February 1998 bin Laden and his associates issued a religious ruling, or *fatwa*, requiring the killing of Americans. They were angry with the United States for fighting Iraq during the Gulf War, for occupying lands on the Arabian Peninsula, and for issuing economic sanctions against Iraq. They viewed the Gulf War as an attempt to destroy Iraq and break up the Middle East. Whether at home or on foreign soil, Americans and those around them were targets of attack.

The bombing of the U.S. Embassy in Nairobi left burning cars *(top inset)* and concrete debris *(bottom inset)* strewn around the damaged building.

THE UNITED STATES EMBASSIES IN KENYA AND TANZANIA

CHAPTER 2

Throughout its history, the U.S. government has recognized the importance of its representation in other countries. Promoting diplomatic relations with other countries has many benefits. Creating opportunities in developing countries abroad means more opportunities at home. Nations can work together to address global problems such as disease, pollution, terrorism, weapon and drug smuggling, and humanitarian crises.

The United States maintains embassies in most of the countries with which it has diplomatic relations. The embassies are usually located in the

TANZANIA AND KENYA AT A GLANCE

United Republic of Tanzania	Republic of Kenya
Population: 37 million	**Population:** 30 million
Capital: Dar es Salaam, pop. 2.8 million (Dodoma is planned as the new national capital)	**Capital:** Nairobi, pop. 1.4 million
Area: 945,090 sq. km (slightly larger than twice the size of California)	**Area:** 582,650 sq. km (slightly smaller than Texas)
Nationality: Tanzanian	**Nationality:** Kenyan
Religions: Christian 45%, Muslim 35%, indigenous beliefs 20%	**Religions:** Protestant 38%, Roman Catholic 28%, indigenous beliefs 26%, Muslim 7%, other 1%
Language: Kiswahili (official), English, Arabic, indigenous languages	**Language:** English (official), Kiswahili (official), more than 40 indigenous languages
Literacy: 67%	**Literacy:** 78%
Life expectancy: 52 years	**Life expectancy:** 47 years
Economy: agriculture 49%, services 34%, industry 17%	**Economy:** services 62%, agriculture 25%, industry 13%
Natural resources: hydropower, tin, phosphates, iron ore, coal, diamonds, gemstones, gold, natural gas, nickel	**Natural resources:** stone, soda ash, salt barites, rubies, fluorspar, garnets, wildlife, hydropower
Government: Republic. Gained independence from Britain in 1961.	**Government:** Republic. Gained independence from Britain in 1963.

host countries' capitals. American embassies are places of cultural exchange and diplomatic efforts. Embassies also handle consular services, such as reviewing passport and visa applications.

Islamic terrorists used a van loaded with 2,000 pounds of explosives to kill sixty-three people at the U.S. Embassy in Beirut, Lebanon, on April 18, 1983.

As cultural and political symbols, embassies have become targets for terrorism. In the mid-1960s, protestors attacked American embassies in response to U.S. involvement in Vietnam. Mobs stoned the embassy in Moscow, Russia, shattering 200 windows. Crowds broke into legations in Budapest, Hungary, and Sofia, Bulgaria, and ripped the great seal of the United States down from both entrances. Terrorists killed three embassy employees in an attack on the U.S. Embassy in Saigon, Vietnam. In the 1970s and 1980s, U.S. embassies continued to be targets. Terrorists attacked American embassies all over the world, including those in Khartoum, Athens, Kuala Lumpur, Tehran, and Beirut.

In 1985, two years after suicide bombers destroyed embassies in Beirut and Kuwait City, Secretary of State

George Shultz appointed Admiral Bobby Inman to head a panel on overseas security. Their study revealed that at least half of the 262 U.S. embassies around the world were unsafe. The panel advised the U.S. government to completely rebuild 75 of the embassies. They wanted some embassies to be moved away from government and city centers in order to make them less vulnerable to attack. The panel recommended that embassies be reconstructed using building materials and architectural designs that would protect them during a bombing.

Congress thought the Inman panel made some wise recommendations. But the $3.5 billion that the panel had requested was too costly. Senate Foreign Relations Chairman Richard Lugar, a Republican from Indiana, accused the State Department of trying to "gold plate" its embassies. In addition, some diplomats and government officials thought that isolating embassies was a bad idea. They believed that embassies should remain public and accessible. They did not want embassies to resemble isolated military fortresses.

Nevertheless, between 1986 and 1990, the State Department requested $2.7 billion to upgrade its embassies. Congress gave much less than had been requested, about $880 million. The State Department made a list of embassies that needed the most protection. Embassies in risky areas like the Middle East and South America were the first to be upgraded.

State Department officials did not think that the embassies at Nairobi, Kenya, and Dar es Salaam, Tanzania, were at risk. The United States enjoys friendly relations with both East African countries. Open since the mid-1960s, the U.S. Embassies in Kenya and Tanzania encourage diplomatic ties and help Americans who live and work in East Africa. The United States's main diplomatic goals in these areas are to help East Africa develop strong economies and democracies. The State Department also wants to prevent the spread of diseases and promote business. Many Kenyans and Tanzanians work alongside State Department employees, offering cultural and language expertise.

The embassies in Nairobi and Dar es Salaam were never renovated to comply with the safety standards recommended by the Inman panel. Some improvements were made, however, and more were planned. In 1988, the State Department spent $750,000 to modify the United States Embassy in Dar es Salaam, including the construction of a nine-foot-high wall around the building. The United States Embassy in Nairobi was scheduled to undergo a $3 million security improvement in January 1999.

The U.S. government made other efforts to improve security. Marines stood guard and steel fences were erected. However, these efforts did not stop terrorists from driving trucks rigged with explosives into the doomed U.S. Embassies one fateful August morning.

Rescuers work by floodlight at the wreckage of the destroyed
U.S. Embassy in Nairobi, Kenya.

THE BOMBINGS

CHAPTER

3

On August 7, 1998, Linda Howard, the personal assistant to Ambassador Prudence Bushnell, was attending a meeting on the fourth floor of the United States Embassy in Nairobi, Kenya. At approximately 10:40 AM she heard a small explosion. Stunned, she and others stood up to see what had happened. Seconds later, an incredible blast shattered every window in the room. Buildings shook as far as ten blocks away. The ceiling started to cave in. Smoke seemed to pour in from every direction.

Embassy guards broke down the door to the meeting

Bystanders help an injured man out of the wreckage of the U.S. Embassy in Nairobi.

room. They shouted for everyone to get down on the floor. Employees dropped to their knees and began crawling out of the room to the stairwell. No one could see. Holding hands, they slowly made their way down the dark staircase. It took fifteen minutes to reach the ground floor. A marine told them to get far away from the building. He worried there might be more explosions.

Shaken, Howard walked to the street. What she saw there frightened her. Burned-out cars and lifeless bodies were everywhere. Buses had been blown apart. People were screaming. Blood covered the streets. Something horrendous had happened, but what?

Bill Barr, director of the U.S. Information Service in Kenya, was also at a meeting in the embassy when it was attacked. Like others, he remembers hearing a thump before the main blast. He thought the thump could have been the sound of a grenade being thrown at the embassy.

Some said there had been gunfire outside the embassy before the big explosion. One witness saw four men jump out of a yellow van parked behind the embassy. One of the men fired into a crowd. The witness thought the men might be robbers, because the embassy was next door to a bank.

The explosion blew the embassy wide open. The blast also toppled the neighboring four-story Ufundi Co-op House and shattered all of the windows in the twenty-two-story Cooperative Bank House. Ambassador Bushnell was in the Cooperative Bank House when the explosion occurred. "I asked was there any construction going on because that's what it sounded like—the kind of boom you hear in construction work. The next thing I knew, I was sitting with my hands over my head," Bushnell told the Associated Press. The ambassador feared the building might collapse. She and others made their way down eighteen flights of stairs. Everyone was bleeding. The railings in the stairwell were wet with blood.

Outside, smoke filled the sky. Flames shot out of buses and cars. Doors were blown off their hinges. Body parts littered the streets. A woman standing across the street from the embassy saw glass and concrete fly into the air and hit people. She saw cars catch on fire. Somehow, she got away.

Mary, a Kenyan employee at the embassy, was knocked off her feet during the blast. She found herself lying at the bottom of a pile of broken chairs and computers. She was covered with a thick liquid and realized it was her own blood. She shouted for help. An American embassy worker uncovered her and helped her leave the building. Many of Mary's co-workers did not make it out. "Most of them who were in that room, most of them are not alive," Mary told Reuters.

Perhaps even more embassy employees in Kenya would have died if the terrorists had been able to reach the building's underground parking lot, as they had planned. Guards had stopped the terrorists from entering the lot, so the terrorists instead detonated the bomb in the parking lot outside. Because the embassy is located at the intersection of two of Nairobi's busiest streets, this twist of fate dealt downtown Nairobi a heavy blow. And because the explosions took place at midmorning, the streets around both embassies were busy. Many people were brutally injured.

The Attack in Tanzania

At virtually the same moment as the explosion in Kenya, a car drove into the residential quarters of the U.S. Embassy in Dar es Salaam, Tanzania. The vehicle exploded, destroying the entrance to the quarters, blowing off chunks of the building's right side, and setting cars on fire. Two-thirds of the building was destroyed. Dar es Salaam's diplomatic quarter was a mess of flame, smoke, and rubble. Trees fell to the ground.

Smoke rises from the U.S. Embassy in Dar es Salaam, Tanzania, as workers gather near a gaping hole in the building.

Seven Tanzanians were killed, and dozens of others were badly hurt. Outside the embassy, a small oil truck lay upside down. It seems likely that a bomb was planted in or on the truck. Right next to the truck was the guardhouse, now a twisted wreck. The guards inside, all of whom might have seen the truck arrive, were dead.

The same bloody scenes that occurred in Nairobi were repeated in Dar es Salaam. A guide had been leading a tour through the Tanzanian embassy. Suddenly, everyone was drenched in blood. Dust and smoke were everywhere. Many people were trapped under heavy filing cabinets. Still others were buried under steel beams and concrete.

PREPARING FOR A BUILDING EXPLOSION

The use of explosives by terrorists can result in collapsed buildings and fires. If you live or work in a multilevel building, you can do the following to increase your chances of survival:

BEFORE

- Review emergency evacuation procedures. Know where fire exits are located.
- Keep fire extinguishers in working order. Know where they are located and how to use them.
- Learn first aid. Contact your local chapter of the American Red Cross for information.
- Keep the following items in a designated place on each floor of the building: portable, battery-operated radio; first-aid kit and manual; several flashlights; extra batteries; several hard hats.

DURING

Get out of the building as quickly and calmly as possible. If items are falling off of bookshelves or from the ceiling, get under a sturdy table or desk. If there is a fire:

- Keep low and exit the building as quickly as possible.
- Cover your nose and mouth with a wet cloth.
- When approaching a closed door, use the palm of your hand and forearm to feel the lower, middle, and upper parts of the door. If it's not too hot, brace yourself against the door and open it slowly. If the door is hot to the touch, do not open it; seek an alternate escape route.
- Smoke and poisonous gases rise, so stay below the smoke at all times.

AFTER

If you are trapped in debris:

- Use a flashlight, if available.
- Stay in your area so that you don't kick up dust. Cover your mouth with a handkerchief or clothing.
- Tap on a pipe or wall so rescuers can hear where you are. Shout only as a last resort—shouting can cause you to inhale dangerous materials.

ASSISTING VICTIMS

Untrained persons should not attempt to rescue people who are inside a collapsed building. Wait for emergency personnel to arrive.

By the end of the day, 224 people from the two embassies were dead, including 12 Americans. More than 4,500 were injured. The scene was so devastating that even trained soldiers were traumatized. Many people were trapped under the rubble of the fallen buildings. Embassy workers walked back and forth near the embassies. They wondered what happened to the people inside. Husbands and wives, sons and daughters, mothers and fathers, and friends wondered if they would ever see their loved ones again.

Many people could not believe that a U.S. embassy—let alone two on the same day—could be attacked and demolished by car bombs. But most people had little time to question the attacks. They knew there were many long days of search and rescue ahead.

Rescuers pull an injured man out of the wreckage of the U.S. Embassy in Nairobi twenty-four hours after the bombing.

THE RESCUE EFFORT

Immediately after the bombings, Red Cross workers, Kenyan and Tanzanian civilians, and American military personnel began a desperate search to find survivors. Volunteers from other countries arrived in East Africa to help in the rescue efforts. Israeli soldiers sifted through the rubble. American medical teams flew in to help in the Kenyan hospitals. FBI agents rushed to the scene to begin their investigation.

Hundreds of people climbed over mountains of rubble and lifted blocks of concrete with pick axes and their bare hands. Officials brought in cranes, back-hoes, and floodlights. At the city hospitals, anyone with the slightest bit of medical knowledge was asked to treat victims. Injured people were brought in to hospitals on makeshift stretchers. Others were treated on the sidewalks. Every time a living person was pulled from the rubble, a cheer went out.

Voices came from the rubble. A secretarial school had been in session on the second floor of the Ufundi Co-op House in Nairobi when it collapsed. A note from the class of twelve was passed out through the ruins. "We are alive," it read. None of the students was heard from again. Nearby, a man buried in the rubble cried for help before he died.

Rose

The tragedy left many sad stories for survivors to tell. One particular story came to symbolize the rescue effort. Rose Wanjiku Mwangi was a clerk at the Ufundi Co-op House. The building collapsed when the bomb exploded, burying her beneath four stories of concrete and steel. A big slab of concrete fell near Rose. It could have killed her. Instead it created a safe hollow, where she waited for someone to find her.

Buried near her was Sammy Ng'ang'a, a business-man who was meeting a partner in the building when it fell. He couldn't see Rose, but he heard her cries for help. Ng'ang'a told Rose not to worry. He heard rescue workers and knew that they would reach them very soon. More than

Lawrence Irungu, Rose Wanjiku Mwangi's husband, waits by the collapsed U.S. Embassy in Nairobi, Kenya, for news of his wife.

twenty-four hours later, on Saturday night, a rescue worker uncovered Ng'ang'a and pulled him to safety. Ng'ang'a said good-bye to Rose and promised that the rescue workers would come for her next.

On Sunday afternoon, Rose called out from the wreckage. She told rescue workers that she needed to go to a hospital. Workers used blowtorches and drills to reach her. They snaked a microphone down to Rose. It helped them figure out where she was. They wanted Rose to know they could hear her, and that help was on the way. Early Monday morning, workers heard a soft clinking noise. It was Rose tapping on concrete to let rescuers know she was still alive.

Meanwhile, Rose's husband, Lawrence Irungu, searched the hospitals and morgue. He had heard that his wife's building had collapsed on Friday. On Tuesday, he learned that a woman named Rose was alive and trapped under the building. Full of hope, Lawrence raced to the disaster site. Two search dogs were leading rescuers to a hole in a heap of rubble. Everyone hoped to find Rose, but the hole was empty.

People worldwide followed Rose's story. Desperate for a sign of hope, they prayed for her safe recovery. Kenya kept a vigil for her. Newspapers called her "Kenya's Rose."

On Wednesday, a crane lifted the last big slab of concrete trapping Rose. Beneath the concrete was a large pile of rubble, wires, and glass. The rescuers worked quickly to remove the debris. Finally, at 3:00 AM, workers uncovered Rose, but she was no longer living. She had died less than twenty-four hours before the rescuers reached her.

The Victims

After a few days, rescue dogs found no more signs of life in the debris in Nairobi. At 10:00 AM on August 12, six days after the bombing, the search for survivors was officially over. To mark the end of the operation, Kenyan, French, Israeli, and U.S. rescue workers held a moment of silence to honor the victims.

Friends and families searched hospitals for loved ones. If they did not find the person they were looking for, they moved on to the morgue. At the morgue, some found the name of their missing person on a list of the dead.

From President Clinton's radio address following the bombings of the U.S. Embassies in Africa, delivered on August 8, 1998:

I want to talk to you about the terrorist bombings that took the lives of Americans and Africans at our embassies in Nairobi, Kenya, and Dar es Salaam, Tanzania. . .

Americans are targets of terrorism, in part, because we have unique leadership responsibilities in the world, because we act to advance peace and democracy, and because we stand united against terrorism.

To change any of that, to pull our diplomats and troops from the world's trouble spots, to turn our backs on those taking risks for peace, to weaken our opposition to terrorism—that would give terrorism a victory it must not and will not have.

The bombs that kill innocent Americans are aimed not only at them, but at the very spirit of our country and the spirit of freedom, for terrorists are the enemies of everything we believe in and fight for: peace and democracy, tolerance and security.

As long as we continue to believe in those values and continue to fight for them, their enemies will not prevail. Our responsibility is great, but the opportunities it brings are even greater.

Many East African civilians died in the attacks. Thousands more were left gravely injured. Douglas Siadolo, twenty-seven, was stuck in traffic outside the Nairobi embassy. When he heard the first explosion, he looked out the window to see what had happened. Siadolo hasn't seen anything since. "My right eye is finished, so they removed it right away," he told the *Los Angeles Times*. "I keep praying they will be able to save my left eye. Right now, I can only make out bright light."

Military pallbearers carry the flag-draped coffins of Americans killed in the bombing of the U.S. Embassy in Nairobi, Kenya.

Because many car and office windows were made of low-quality glass that shattered easily, there are hundreds of stories like Siadolo's. Shards of glass were even found in people's lungs. Like Siadolo, people rushed to their windows when the grenade exploded to see what happened. Moments later, when the car bomb detonated, they were caught staring straight into a rain of glass. The explosion was the worst single contributor to blindness in Kenya's history.

The national emergency created hundreds of personal emergencies. Many Kenyans worried about how they would pay funeral costs. A funeral can cost thousands of dollars, and Kenya is a country where most people have average annual incomes of $270. Many people lost relatives who had supported their entire families.

Eleven flag-draped coffins were flown back to the United States for burial. The body of a twelfth American victim had been shipped back earlier. The Americans who worked at the Kenyan and Tanzanian embassies had dedicated their lives to public service. Some who died, like Julian Bartley, were career diplomats. Bartley was a foreign service official from Brooklyn, New York. His son Jay, twenty years old, died with him during the attack. Others worked for the military, like twenty-one-year-old Marine Sergeant Jesse Aliganga and Air Force Master Sergeant Sherry Olds. Mary Louise Martin was a scientist working to treat drug-resistant strains of malaria. Like hundreds of others who died in the bombings, the work and lives of these United States citizens were cut short.

Seeking clues about the bombing, FBI and Kenyan investigators comb the wreckage of the U.S. Embassy in Nairobi.

THE INVESTIGATION

After the embassy bombings, investigators had a mystery to unravel. Were the bombings a reaction to U.S. policy in Africa? Or were terrorists from other countries staging a war in Africa?

Many investigators suspected that Islamic terrorists had targeted Americans on foreign soil. Neither Kenya nor Tanzania had histories of international terrorist attacks. Compared with other African countries, in Kenya and Tanzania foreigners can come and go with relative ease. Maybe these were the reasons that terrorists targeted these two embassies in particular.

The Attack Against the U.S. Embassies in Kenya and Tanzania

The Kenyan and Tanzanian governments controlled the crime scenes. They helped FBI agents gather evidence. Agents brought in plastic and paper bags, gloves, fingerprint kits, brooms, shovels, cotton swabs, toothbrushes, cameras, and picks. They used these tools to carefully search every inch of the crime scenes.

Investigators interviewed people about what they saw. There were many eyewitness accounts. One U.S. Embassy official thought the vehicle containing the bomb had been driven to the Nairobi embassy's main entrance first. The guards sent the driver to the rear of the building, where the bomb exploded. Some witnesses reported that a hand grenade was used to kill guards at the rear entrance. The main bomb exploded after that attack.

A man working for the Kenyan environmental ministry said he saw two men drive a yellow pickup truck to the back of the embassy and jump out with machine guns. The witness said one man ran back into the vehicle while the other shot bullets into the embassy.

Other witnesses saw a man drive a pickup truck into the parking lot. The man sat quietly in the truck until it exploded. Experts say the vehicle bomb probably contained as much as 600 pounds of explosives.

At the U.S. Embassy in Tanzania, investigators focused on a blue water-delivery tanker that drew up to the embassy gates in Dar es Salaam shortly before it exploded.

FBI special agent Sheila Horan tells the press about the investigation of five Islamic terrorists suspected in the bombing of the U.S. Embassies in Nairobi, Kenya, and Dar es Salaam, Tanzania.

Finding the Suspects

A group calling itself the Islamic Army for the Liberation of Holy Places claimed responsibility for the bombings the day after the attacks. The U.S. State Department would not confirm that the group was in fact responsible. Sometimes after a terrorist attack, groups phone in to falsely claim responsibility.

There had been no warning of the attacks beforehand. But terrorism experts thought a known terrorist group from outside Africa picked the embassies in Kenya and Tanzania because security might be lax and, possibly, because Kenya and Tanzania are relatively close to the Middle East. Those responsible were not amateurs. The twin attacks were well planned and carried out.

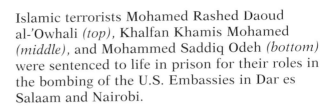

Islamic terrorists Mohamed Rashed Daoud al-'Owhali *(top)*, Khalfan Khamis Mohamed *(middle)*, and Mohammed Saddiq Odeh *(bottom)* were sentenced to life in prison for their roles in the bombing of the U.S. Embassies in Dar es Salaam and Nairobi.

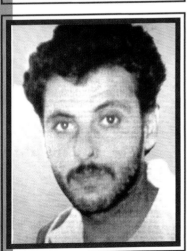

Unofficially, U.S. law enforcement and intelligence officials linked the bombings to an Egyptian terrorist group financed by the infamous Osama bin Laden. In July, the group had warned that it was preparing to attack American targets. Bin Laden had already issued a fatwa against Americans. He had organizations in East Africa and the money to orchestrate such an attack.

U.S. intelligence officials looked at electronic messages from bin Laden's communications network. They found evidence that bin Laden had helped plan the attacks. They also found congratulatory messages about the "success" of the bombings in Nairobi and Dar es Salaam.

The bombs used in the attacks were similar to some used in the past by the Egyptian Islamic Jihad group. Officials also said the leaders of the Egyptian Islamic Jihad group had recently

AL QAEDA

Al Qaeda means "the base." It is a network of militant Islamic groups created in the late 1980s by Osama bin Laden. A council of members from around the world governs al Qaeda. Bin Laden is thought to lead the council. Over twenty-four groups belong to al Qaeda. They include:

Armed Islamic Group, Algeria
Islamic Jihad, Egypt
Hezbollah, Lebanon
Islamic Movement of Uzbekistan, Uzbekistan
Harkat ul-Mujahedin, Kashmir
Moro Islamic Liberation Front, Philippines

joined bin Laden at his camp in Afghanistan. U.S. satellites showed that bin Laden moved his camps in Afghanistan immediately after the attacks. Were bin Laden and his associates trying to hide? The evidence did not prove that bin Laden or his associates were guilty. But it added to growing suspicions.

A Confession

Investigators warned that it would not be easy to pin down the group or country behind the bombings. Even so, the FBI had many leads. One person told police to investigate a suspicious man named Mohamed Rashed Daoud al-'Owhali, a twenty-four-year-old Saudi. When investigators found al-'Owhali, he was covered with cuts. He claimed to be an innocent victim of the bombings. Investigators were not convinced.

FBI TEN MOST WANTED FUGITIVE

**MURDER OF U.S. NATIONALS OUTSIDE THE UNITED STATES;
CONSPIRACY TO MURDER U.S. NATIONALS OUTSIDE THE UNITED STATES;
ATTACK ON A FEDERAL FACILITY RESULTING IN DEATH**

USAMA BIN LADEN

Date of Photograph Unknown

Aliases: Usama Bin Muhammad Bin Ladin, Shaykh Usama Bin Ladin, the Prince, the Emir, Abu Abdallah, Mujahid Shaykh, Hajj, the Director

DESCRIPTION

Date of Birth:	1957		**Hair:**	Brown
Place of Birth:	Saudi Arabia		**Eyes:**	Brown
Height:	6' 4" to 6' 6"		**Complexion:**	Olive
Weight:	Approximately 160 pounds		**Sex:**	Male
Build:	Thin		**Nationality:**	Saudi Arabian
Occupation(s):	Unknown			
Remarks:	He is the leader of a terrorist organization known as Al-Qaeda "The Base." He walks with a cane.			

CAUTION

USAMA BIN LADEN IS WANTED IN CONNECTION WITH THE AUGUST 7, 1998, BOMBINGS OF THE UNITED STATES EMBASSIES IN DAR ES SALAAM, TANZANIA AND NAIROBI, KENYA. THESE ATTACKS KILLED OVER 200 PEOPLE.

CONSIDERED ARMED AND EXTREMELY DANGEROUS

IF YOU HAVE ANY INFORMATION CONCERNING THIS PERSON, PLEASE CONTACT YOUR LOCAL FBI OFFICE OR THE NEAREST U.S. EMBASSY OR CONSULATE.

REWARD

The United States Government is offering a reward of up to $5 million for information leading directly to the apprehension or conviction of Usama Bin Laden.

www.fbi.gov

May 1999

As the man responsible for the murders of thousands of innocent people, Osama bin Laden is one of the most wanted terrorists in world history.

Investigators got more lucky breaks. A suspect named Mohammed Saddiq Odeh was arrested in Pakistan for using a phony passport. Odeh, a thirty-six-year-old from Jordan, was brought back to Kenya. At first, he denied any involvement in the bombings. Later, he confessed, spilling many details about the attack. He identified other men linked to the bombings, including al-'Owhali; Khalfan Khamis Mohamed, a twenty-seven-year-old Tanzanian and explosives expert; and Wadih el-Hage, a forty-year-old American citizen born in Lebanon. Most important, Odeh said their group was part of the al Qaeda network headed by Osama bin Laden.

The State Department offered a $5 million reward for the arrest of bin Laden. The FBI put bin Laden on its list of the ten most wanted criminals. The U.S. government wanted to bring him to trial on charges of killing American civilians and soldiers, including those killed in the African embassy bombings. But bin Laden proved difficult to find. He was believed to be hiding in the mountains of Afghanistan with the help and support of Afghanistan's Taliban government. Although bin Laden had issued a fatwa calling for the killing of all Americans, he denied any direct involvement in the attacks.

In December 1998, the Justice Department charged Odeh, al-'Owhali, Mohamed, el-Hage, and bin Laden with conspiracy to commit murder in the embassy bombings.

In this courtroom sketch, the defendants in the embassy bombings listen as prosecutors deliver opening statements at their trial in New York City.

THE TRIAL AND THE SENTENCING

CHAPTER 6

After a three-year investigation that cost millions of dollars, in January 2001, the federal government brought four men to trial for the African embassy bombings. They were Mohammed Saddiq Odeh, Mohamed Rashed Daoud al-'Owhali, Khalfan Khamis Mohamed, and Wadih el-Hage. Additional men had also been charged, including Osama bin Laden. Some of those men were in hiding or had taken refuge in other countries and could not be brought to court.

Still, people were glad to see the case go to trial. "This is an important step in our fight against terrorism," Attorney General Janet Reno told Americans. "It sends a message that no terrorist can flout our laws and murder innocent victims."

If convicted, Mohamed and al-'Owhali faced the death penalty. Mohamed was accused of preparing TNT for the bomb that destroyed the U.S. Embassy in Dar es Salaam. Al-'Owhali was accused of helping transport the bomb. Officials said al-'Owhali helped load the bomb onto a truck and then rode the truck partway to the embassy. The two men had confessed their crimes to American investigators in Kenya. Later, their attorneys argued that the confessions should be thrown out. They argued that their clients' Miranda rights had been violated because they had not been allowed to talk to lawyers before they confessed.

The two other men, Odeh and el-Hage, faced life sentences if convicted. They were charged with working for the al Qaeda terrorist group. Odeh's and el-Hage's attorneys said that their clients worked for bin Laden, but had done nothing criminal.

The Trial

Inside the Manhattan courthouse, one witness, Jamal Ahmed al-Fadl, talked about life as an Islamic warrior with bin Laden. Al-Fadl's English was not polished. He was nervous. But his words were clear: Bin Laden had told him and many others that America was a snake and must be killed.

These chunks of damaged metal were among the many exhibits entered into evidence at the embassy bombings trial.

In his closing arguments, a prosecutor told the jury about Rose Wanjiku Mwangi, the woman who lay trapped in the rubble of the bombed Kenyan embassy for days before she died. "Her life was lost; her life was taken from her," the prosecutor told the jury. He said Rose symbolized the senseless, brutal killing of all the people who had died that day. He asked the jury to convict the four men.

In July 2001, all four men were convicted. The jury then had to decide what sentence the men would receive. Prosecutors thought the two men directly involved in the bombing, al-'Owhali and Mohamed, should receive death sentences. In the U.S. court system, the sentence of death requires the unanimous vote of all twelve jurors. A few jurors did not want to impose the death sentence. They did not want the men to become martyrs. They worried others might use the men's deaths as an excuse to commit more acts of terrorism. Instead, all four defendants were sentenced to life in prison.

The men who were sentenced were low- to mid-level members of the Islamic militant group al Qaeda. They were just a few of those who were charged with the bombing. Those who were most responsible, such as bin Laden, remained at large.

Doreen Mutai, a Kenyan woman, came to New York to watch the trial. When the men were sentenced, Mutai, whose husband was killed in the Kenyan bombing, said the trial and sentencing made no difference. "Terrorism is still there," she told the Associated Press. "The bombing is still there. Nothing can be done about these fanatics. We don't even know their cause."

The Aftermath

For weeks after the attack on the embassies, bulldozers rumbled through debris. U.S. Marines stood guard at the bombed-out buildings, machine guns in hand. An American flag flew at half-mast. Outside the embassy in Nairobi, Kenyans laid piles of roses and carnations. They posted signs. "Kenyans Want Peace, Not Bombs," read one sign. "God Heal the Heavy Hearts," read another.

A controversial result of the bombings was the attack launched by the United States against bin Laden before he was even announced as a suspect. In retaliation, the United States launched missiles against targets in Afghanistan and Sudan. The missiles were directed at terrorist training camps supposedly

Kenyans gather at the site of the U.S. Embassy in Nairobi for a memorial service on the first anniversary of the terrorist bombing.

run by bin Laden. At the time, bin Laden was believed to be hiding in Afghanistan and protected by Afghanistan's fundamentalist Muslim government, the Taliban. "Today, we have struck back," President Clinton told Americans.

But the missiles were either misdirected or had not fallen when they were supposed to. One missile that did hit as planned struck a medicine factory in Sudan. U.S. sources believed the factory was actually making chemical weapons and was somehow tied to bin Laden. When this proved false, the owner of the factory sued the U.S. government. The owner wanted compensation for the damage and said that the United States had no foundation for assuming chemical weapons were being manufactured there.

The fundamentalist Muslim Taliban is thought to have harbored Osama bin Laden after the embassy attacks.

The United States spent $79 million on the missiles, which destroyed only a few thousand dollars worth of tents. Only one of the camps hit was thought to be an actual bin Laden terrorist training camp. To make matters worse, the attacks frightened and angered many Islamic countries.

The missiles killed many, but bin Laden wasn't one of them. Years later, bin Laden would be the chief suspect in the terrorist attacks of September 11, 2001. The U.S. government redoubled its efforts to find him. At the time that this book was printed, his whereabouts were still unknown.

The bombings at the embassies in Dar es Salaam and Nairobi had long-lasting effects. Many people suffered from severe depression, panic, and other psychological disorders. Some survivors thought about the bombings over and over again. For some, every loud noise they heard was another possible car bomb. Some were so traumatized they refused to leave their apartments. Hundreds of minds and bodies were disabled by the bombings.

A counseling operation helped some traumatized patients. The counseling was funded in part by a $37 million grant the U.S. Congress gave to Kenya after the bombing. Tanzania received $9 million. Most of the money given to Kenya went toward helping rebuild office buildings that were destroyed in the explosions.

Deeper Destruction

Before the bombing, Tanzania was one of few countries in Africa that had known peace. Its inhabitants pride themselves on their peaceful nature. The name of Tanzania's capital, Dar es Salaam, means "haven of peace."

The serene feeling of peace was shattered by the 1998 attack. American diplomats began to worry about being attacked in countries that had friendly relations with the United States. Security tightened at U.S. embassies and military installations around the world.

The attacks left some Kenyans with a negative view of the United States. They thought Americans did not help Kenyans in the hours following the explosions. They said Americans worried only about protecting themselves and did not help local people. When Kenyan locals wanted to help rescue victims trapped beneath the embassy rubble, U.S. Marines would not let them (or anyone) enter the bombed embassy. The U.S. ambassador later explained that the marines were guarding the embassy from looters. This was

The names of the 219 people killed in the U.S. Embassy bombing in Nairobi, Kenya, are engraved on this memorial monument, which was built on the site of the destruction.

an insult to Kenyans, who only wanted to help. Looting was the furthest thing from their minds.

Some Kenyans were upset when the U.S. State Department issued a travel warning after the explosion. The warning advised travelers to stay away from Kenya for reasons of safety, but the Kenyan government worried that its economy, which relies on tourism, would be hurt by the warning. The State Department did not want Kenya and Tanzania to be punished as a result of the attacks, so it quickly withdrew the advisory. Even so, the embassy bombings kept many travelers from visiting East Africa. Travel bookings in the months following the attack were down 70 percent. Many large beachfront hotels were forced to close.

Although the bombings were attacks on Americans, ordinary Kenyans and Tanzanians were also victims and heroes of the tragedy. They selflessly plunged into the rubble and worked day and night to find survivors. Workers labored beside schoolchildren. Men made bandages from their own shirts. Thousands donated blood. Kenya's President Daniel arap Moi arrived at the scene with leaders of opposing political parties to help and comfort victims. People worked side by side in an effort to help those in need. It was an unselfish display of strength and unity.

Before the 1998 bombings, Kenya and Tanzania had no history of international terrorism. The bombings made the United States government think much more about the security of places in which it previously had felt safe. The bombings were a sad reminder that terrorism can strike anywhere, at any time.

On August 7, 2001, three years after the attack, Memorial Park officially opened in Nairobi, Kenya. The park was built on the site where the U.S. Embassy once had stood. The peaceful park features a fountain, benches, and a sculpture made out of some of the wreckage left over from the explosion. Once a scene of torn bodies and shattered buildings, the grassy square is now a place to reflect and remember.

GLOSSARY

Allah   Arabic word for God.

ally   A nation with whom another nation has a friendly association.

anarchist   A person who rebels against authority, often using violent means.

colonialism   A policy by which a nation extends control over a foreign nation.

consular   An official who lives in a foreign country, representing his or her own country's interests and helping its citizens there.

crusader   A person who sets upon a vigorous campaign or mission.

diplomat   A person who deals with relations between two countries, working for one country while living in another.

exile   Forced absence from one's country.

extremist   One who advocates measures beyond the norm.

fatwa   An Islamic religious opinion, sometimes a ruling.

fundamentalist   A person who strictly follows the practices and beliefs of a religion.

Islam   The predominant religion in the Middle East and much of Asia whose followers are called Muslims.

jihad   A holy war waged on behalf of Islam.

Koran   The sacred text of Islam, considered by Muslims to contain God's revelations to Mohammed.

legation   A diplomatic mission in a foreign country ranking below an embassy.

martyr   A person who suffers death for a cause, often drawing more sympathy to the cause.

Miranda rights   A warning given to a criminal suspect upon arrest, informing him or her of the right to have an attorney present during any interrogation.

Mohammed   The Arab prophet of Islam.

mosque   A Muslim house of worship.

Muslim   A follower of Islam.

regime   A system or government.

sanction   A penalty to ensure obedience to the law.

terrorism   The unlawful use or threatened use of force or violence by a person or group against people or property in order to intimidate or coerce. Often enacted for ideological or political reasons.

FOR MORE INFORMATION

American Red Cross National Headquarters
430 17th Street NW
Washington, DC 20006
(202) 728-6400
Web site: http://www.redcross.org

Anti-Defamation League
823 United Nations Plaza
New York, NY 10017
(212) 490-2525
Web site: http://www.adl.org

U.S. State Department
2201 C Street NW
Washington, DC 20520
(202) 647-4000
Web site: http://www.state.gov

Due to the changing nature of Internet links, the Rosen
Publishing Group, Inc., has developed an online list of
Web sites related to the subject of this book. This site is
updated regularly. Please use this link to access the list:
http://www.rosenlinks.com/tat/aaus/

For Further Reading

Egendorf, Laura K., ed. *Terrorism: Opposing Viewpoints.*
San Diego: Greenhaven Press, 2000.

Harris, Jonathan. *The New Terrorism: Politics of
Violence.* New York: Julian Messner, 1983.

Henderson, Harry. *Terrorism.* New York: Facts
on File, 2001.

Marcovitz, Hal. *Terrorism.* Philadelphia: Chelsea House
Publishers, 2001.

Streissguth, Thomas. *International Terrorists.*
Minneapolis, MN: The Oliver Press, Inc., 1993.

Weinberg, Leonard, and Paul Davis. *Introduction to
Political Terrorism.* New York: McGraw-Hill, 1989.

Whittaker, David J., ed. *The Terrorism Reader.* New York:
Routledge, 2001.

BIBLIOGRAPHY

Alexander, Yonah, David Carlton, and Paul Wilkinson. *Terrorism: Theory and Practice*. Boulder, CO: Westview Press, 1979.

Barnaby, Frank. *Instruments of Terror*. London: Vision Paperbacks, 1996.

Combs, Cindy C. *Terrorism in the Twenty-First Century*. Upper Saddle River, NJ: Prentice Hall, 2000.

Crenshaw, Martha, ed. *Terrorism, Legitimacy, and Power: The Consequences of Political Violence*. Middletown, CT: Wesleyan University Press, 1983.

Egendorf, Laura K., ed. *Terrorism: Opposing Viewpoints*. San Diego: Greenhaven Press, 2000.

Evans, Ernest. *Calling a Truce to Terror: The American Response to International Terrorism*. Westport, CT: Greenwood Press, 1979.

Fitzpatrick, Mary. *Tanzania, Zanzibar & Pemba*. Berkeley, CA: Lonely Planet, 1999.

Harris, Jonathan. *The New Terrorism: Politics of Violence*. New York: Julian Messner, 1983.

Henderson, Harry. *Terrorism*. New York: Facts on File, Inc., 2001.

Hoffman, David. *The Oklahoma City Bombing and the Politics of Terror.* Venice, CA: Feral House, 1998.

Juergensmeyer, Mark. *Terror in the Mind of God.* Berkeley, CA: University of California Press, 2000.

Loeffler, Jane C. *The Architecture of Diplomacy: Building America's Embassies.* New York: Princeton Architectural Press, 1998.

Marcovitz, Hal. *Terrorism.* Philadelphia: Chelsea House Publishers, 2001.

Schreiber, Jan. *The Ultimate Weapon: Terrorists and World Order.* New York: William Morrow & Co., 1978.

Streissguth, Thomas. *International Terrorists.* Minneapolis, MN: The Oliver Press Inc., 1993.

Sullivan, Joseph, ed. *Embassies Under Siege: Personal Accounts by Diplomats on the Front Line.* London: Brassey's, 1995.

Wardlaw, Grant. *Political Terrorism: Theory, Tactics, and Counter-measures.* New York: Cambridge University Press, 1982.

Whittaker, David J., eds. *The Terrorism Reader.* New York: Routledge, 2001.

Weinberg, Leonard, and Paul Davis. *Introduction to Political Terrorism.* New York: McGraw-Hill, 1989.

INDEX

About the Author

Amanda Ferguson is a freelance writer living in Los Angeles.

Photo Credits

Cover, pp. 8–9, 16, 27, 51 © Sayyid Azim/AP Wide World Photos; p. 6 © Dave Caulkin/AP Wide World Photos; p. 10 © Barry Iverson/TimePix; pp. 12, 19 42 (middle and bottom) © AP Wide World Photos; pp. 15, 46–47 © Reuters/TimePix; pp. 22–23, 38–39 © John McConnico/AP Wide World Photos; p. 24 © George Mulala/TimePix; pp. 30–31 © Ken Karuga/AP Wide World Photos; pp. 33, 54 © Jean-Marc Bouju/AP Wide World Photos; p. 36 © Dirck Halstead/TimePix; p. 41 © Khalil Senosi/AP Wide World Photos; p. 42 (top) © *Daily Nation*/AP Wide World Photos; p. 44 © Federal Bureau of Investigation/AP Wide World Photos; p. 49 © Robert Mecea/AP Wide World Photos; p. 52 © Gleb Garanich/TimePix.

Editor

Christine Poolos

Series Design and Layout

Geri Giordano